TODAY'S WOMEN'S FASHION

Women's fashion is an evolving art form

Q. BANKS

Table of Contents

Introduction

Ladies' style is a continually developing industry that includes clothing, frill, footwear, and cosmetics. It is impacted by different variables, including social patterns, social convictions, and individual inclinations. Ladies' design envelops many styles, from easygoing wear to formal clothing.

Some famous ladies' design styles include:

Bohemian: portrayed by streaming textures, botanical prints, and baggy attire.

Exemplary: immortal and rich apparel, like custom fitted suits, minimal dark dresses, and pearls.

Streetwear: impacted by metropolitan culture, described by curiously large apparel, shoes, and strong realistic plans.

Preppy: motivated by Elite level style, portrayed by clean lines, stripes, and exemplary examples.

Stylish: described by shimmering textures, high heels, and proclamation gems.

Lively: agreeable and practical apparel, like tights, tennis shoes, and athleisure wear.

Ladies' design likewise incorporates different frill, like purses, gems, caps, and scarves, which can be utilized to improve and supplement an outfit. Lately, maintainable and moral style has become progressively significant in the business, with numerous fashioners and brands zeroing in on making earth cognizant and socially capable dress.

Bohemian

Bohemian style is a style that has its foundations in the Bohemian culture of the nineteenth hundred years. It is portrayed by a loose and unique look, with an accentuation on normal materials, gritty varieties, and streaming textures. The Bohemian style is about independence and imagination, and it embraces a large number of impacts, from Eastern and African societies to classic and retro styles.

The expression "Bohemian" initially alluded to individuals who carried on with an offbeat way of life, frequently including creative or scholarly pursuits. Bohemians dismissed the severe normal practices of their time and on second thought embraced a more lighthearted and non-traditionalist lifestyle. This way of life was frequently connected with neediness, as numerous Bohemians were craftsmen, performers, or scholars who battled to earn enough to pay the bills from their work.

The Bohemian style of dress was an augmentation of this non-traditionalist way of life. It dismissed the firm and formal attire of the high societies for agreeable and viable apparel that took into consideration opportunity of development. This included baggy shirts and pullovers, streaming skirts and dresses, and agreeable footwear like shoes and sandals.

The Bohemian style is described by many materials, from normal strands like cotton, cloth, and silk to additional outlandish materials like calfskin, softened cowhide, and fur. The utilization of normal materials is a significant piece of the Bohemian stylish, as it mirrors the development's accentuation on living as one with nature.

The shades of the Bohemian style are likewise vital. Hearty tones like brown, beige, and green are frequently utilized, as are more brilliant varieties like red, orange, and turquoise. The utilization of examples and prints is likewise normal, with flower prints, paisley designs, and mathematical plans being well known decisions.

Frill are a significant piece of the Bohemian style, with many choices accessible. Adornments is frequently produced using regular materials like wood, globules, and plumes, and is intended to look rural and carefully assembled. Scarves, caps, and headbands are additionally well known, frequently highlighting beautiful prints or weaving.

As of late, the Bohemian style has encountered a resurgence in fame, with many style creators and retailers offering dress and frill that mirror the style's unique and capricious ethos. The present Bohemian design incorporates many styles, from easygoing and happy with attire to additional formal and exquisite plans.

One of the critical components of the advanced Bohemian style is layering. This includes wearing various layers of dress to make an extraordinary and individual look. For instance, a normal Bohemian outfit could incorporate a streaming maxi dress, a denim coat, and a bright scarf or cloak.

One more significant component of the cutting edge Bohemian style is the utilization of one of a kind or retro dress. Numerous Bohemian fashionistas shop at secondhand shops or online classic shops to find remarkable and stand-out pieces that mirror their singular style.

The Bohemian style is likewise firmly connected with live performances, where participants frequently dress in a lighthearted and eccentric manner. This has prompted the ascent of the "celebration style" pattern, which consolidates numerous components of the Bohemian style, including flowy dresses, periphery, and botanical prints.

All in all, the Bohemian style is a style that has its foundations in the Bohemian culture of the nineteenth 100 years. It is portrayed by a loose and unique look, with an accentuation on regular materials, hearty tones, and streaming textures. The

Bohemian style is about distinction and inventiveness, and it embraces a great many impacts, from Eastern and African societies to rare and retro styles. The present Bohemian design incorporates a wide

Classic

Exemplary style in design is an immortal and rich approach to dressing that underlines straightforwardness, quality, and complexity. Exemplary style is frequently connected with conventional fitting, clean lines, and nonpartisan tones. A style has been stylish for a really long time and stays famous today because of its immortal allure.

The exemplary style is frequently connected with the privileged societies and formal events. A style radiates certainty, power, and tastefulness. Exemplary style isn't just about wearing the most recent patterns, however about putting resources into quality pieces that will endure forever. The attention is on downplayed extravagance, with an accentuation on textures, cut, and development.

One of the signs of the exemplary style is the little dark dress. This straightforward, exquisite piece of clothing was promoted by Coco Chanel during the 1920s and has been a staple of ladies' closets from that point onward. The little dark dress is flexible and can be spruced up or down relying upon the event. It is an ideal illustration of the exemplary style, as it is both immortal and modern.

One more key component of the exemplary style is fitting. Exemplary apparel is frequently produced using great materials like fleece, silk, and cashmere, and is intended to fit well and

compliment the body. Fitting is an art that requires expertise and tender loving care, and the best exemplary dress is made by gifted tailors who have consummated their art over numerous years.

Exemplary style is additionally described by nonpartisan varieties like dark, white, dim, and naval force. These tones are ageless and adaptable, and they can be effectively joined with different varieties and examples. Exemplary attire is intended to be worn for a long time, so it is critical that the varieties are immortal and won't leave design.

Extras are additionally a significant piece of the exemplary style. Exemplary extras are basic and exquisite, like a pearl necklace, a calfskin purse, or a couple of cowhide gloves. Exemplary embellishments are intended to supplement the outfit, not overwhelm it. They are frequently produced using top notch materials like cowhide, gold, or silver, and are intended to endure forever.

The exemplary style isn't only for ladies. Men's exemplary style is portrayed by custom fitted suits, fresh shirts, and cleaned shoes. The emphasis is on quality materials and magnificent fitting. Men's exemplary style is immortal and refined, and it is frequently connected with power and authority.

One of the vital advantages of the exemplary style is that it is immortal. Exemplary dress never leaves design, so putting resources into a couple of key pieces can set aside cash over the long haul. Exemplary apparel is additionally flexible, as it tends to be spruced up or down relying upon the event. Exemplary dress is intended to endure, so it is in many cases more costly than quick style. Be that as it may, it merits the speculation, as exemplary attire will keep going for a long time and will continuously look polished.

All in all, the exemplary style is an immortal and rich approach to dressing that stresses effortlessness, quality, and refinement. The attention is on downplayed extravagance, with an accentuation on textures, cut, and development. The exemplary style isn't just about wearing the most recent patterns, yet about putting resources into quality pieces that will endure forever. A style radiates certainty, power, and tastefulness, and it is frequently connected with conventional fitting, clean lines, and unbiased varieties. Exemplary dress never leaves style, and enduring forever is flexible and planned.

Streetwear

Streetwear is a design style that began from the metropolitan culture of the US during the 1980s. It has since spread all over the planet, and it is presently a worldwide peculiarity. Streetwear is described by its easygoing and happy with attire, frequently including intense illustrations, splendid tones, and expressive plans. It is a design style that is related with youth culture, hip-bounce, and skating.

The expression "streetwear" was first utilized during the 1990s to portray the design style that was famous among metropolitan youth. Streetwear is a combination of various styles, including skating, hip-jump, troublemaker, and Japanese road design. A style is continually developing and impacted by various societies and subcultures.

Streetwear is frequently connected with the hip-jump culture, as numerous rappers and hip-bounce craftsmen wear streetwear clothing in their music recordings and exhibitions. This has assisted with promoting the streetwear style all over the planet. Skating is likewise a huge impact on streetwear, as many skating brands have become inseparable from the style.

The vital highlights of streetwear clothing are solace, usefulness, and style. Streetwear clothing is intended to be agreeable and useful, as it is frequently worn for regular exercises, for example, skating or spending time with companions. The attire is produced using excellent materials that are solid and ready to endure mileage.

One of the most unmistakable elements of streetwear is the utilization of realistic plans and logos. Streetwear clothing frequently includes strong illustrations, splendid tones, and expressive plans that say something. These plans are many times propelled by mainstream society, music, and recent developments. Streetwear marks frequently team up with craftsmen and creators to make remarkable and eye-getting plans.

Streetwear likewise puts a huge accentuation on tennis shoes. Shoes are a critical component of the streetwear style, and they are many times worn as a proclamation piece. Tennis shoes are intended to be both snazzy and agreeable, and they are frequently produced using great materials. Tennis shoe culture is a huge piece of the streetwear local area, and there are numerous tennis shoe occasions and shows held all over the planet.

One more significant component of streetwear is the utilization of extras. Streetwear adornments incorporate caps, rucksacks, shades, and gems. These adornments are frequently intended to supplement the attire and complete the general look. Streetwear frill are frequently produced using great materials and component remarkable plans.

Streetwear has turned into a worldwide peculiarity, with numerous streetwear brands acquiring prevalence all over the planet. The absolute most well known streetwear brands incorporate Incomparable, Bape, Royal residence, Grayish, and Stüssy. These brands have become inseparable from the streetwear style, and their apparel and frill are exceptionally pursued.

One of the advantages of streetwear is its inclusivity. Streetwear is a style that is embraced by individuals of any age and foundations. A style commends singularity and self-articulation. Streetwear isn't just about pursuing the most recent directions, however about making an extraordinary and individual style.

All in all, streetwear is a design style that began from the metropolitan culture of the US during the 1980s. It is portrayed by its easygoing and happy with attire, frequently including intense illustrations, brilliant varieties, and expressive plans. Streetwear is a combination of various styles, including skating, hip-bounce, troublemaker, and Japanese road design. A style is continually developing and impacted by various societies and subcultures. Streetwear puts a huge accentuation on tennis shoes and embellishments, and a style is embraced by individuals of any age and foundations.

Preppy

Preppy design is a style that arose during the 1950s and 60s in the US, basically among the understudies of tip top colleges like Harvard, Yale, and Princeton. The preppy style is portrayed by its spotless and exemplary appearance, with an emphasis on quality and customary dress things. The style became famous among privileged youth and has since turned into a broadly perceived and regarded style.

Preppy clothing is characterized by its work of art and immortal nature, with an accentuation on conventional things, for example, polo shirts, conservative Oxford shirts, and khaki jeans. The varieties are regularly muffled and stifled, with an inclination for naval force blue, white, and pastel shades. The dress is intended to be agreeable and useful, with an emphasis on excellent materials like cotton, fleece, and cashmere.

The preppy style is known for its utilization of exemplary examples like plaids, stripes, and polka specks. These examples are many times seen on shirts, ties, and skirts, and they are utilized to add visual interest to in any case basic attire things. The examples are regularly quelled and downplayed, with an inclination for quieted tones and limited scope plans.

Extras are a significant piece of preppy design, and they are utilized to supplement the apparel and complete the general look. For men, extras frequently incorporate belts, watches, and loafers, while ladies might wear pearl neckbands, headbands, and artful dance pads. These adornments are frequently produced using excellent materials like cowhide and gold, and they are intended to be immortal and durable.

The preppy style is likewise characterized by its utilization of athletic apparel, with an emphasis on exemplary things, for example, tennis skirts, deck shoes, and polo shirts. These things are normally produced using lightweight materials and are intended to be both useful and popular. The athletic apparel part of preppy style has its foundations in the Elite level colleges, where understudies would wear activewear for their everyday exercises.

One of the vital elements of preppy style is its accentuation on custom and legacy. Numerous preppy clothing things have a long history and are related with a specific culture or way of life. For instance, the polo shirt was initially worn by polo players in the late nineteenth 100 years, while the deck shoe was intended for mariners during the 1930s. These things have since become inseparable from the preppy style and are viewed as fundamental bits of a preppy closet.

The preppy style has advanced over the long run and has consolidated components from other style. For instance, during the 1980s, preppy design was affected by the prominence of force dressing, with ladies wearing shoulder braces and men brandishing curiously large overcoats. Nonetheless, the center components of preppy design have continued as before, with an emphasis on quality, custom, and exemplary dress things.

Today, preppy style is as yet well known among youthful grown-ups and is frequently connected with a specific way of life and mentality. Preppy style is viewed as a method for conveying a feeling of refinement and class, while likewise being agreeable and down to earth. The preppy style has likewise turned into a well known decision for the people who esteem manageability and moral style, as the emphasis on quality and solidness implies that preppy clothing things are intended to keep going for a long time.

All in all, preppy design is a style that arose in the US during the 1950s and 60s among the understudies of world class colleges. The preppy style is described by its perfect and exemplary appearance, with an emphasis on quality and customary dress things. Preppy clothing is characterized by its work of art and ageless nature, with an accentuation on customary things, for example, polo shirts, traditional Oxford shirts, and khaki jeans. Extras are a significant piece of preppy design, and they are utilized to supplement the dress and complete the general look.

Glamorous

Captivating design is a style that radiates tastefulness and refinement, with an emphasis on extravagant textures, embellishments, and frill. The style arose during the 1920s during the brilliant time of Hollywood and has since turned into a well known style.

The sign of alluring style is its accentuation on great materials and rich completions. Clothing things are regularly produced using very good quality textures like silk, glossy silk, and velvet, and they frequently include embellishments like sequins, globules, and quills. The dress is intended to be perfectly sized and figure-complimenting, with an emphasis on featuring the bends of the body.

Captivating design likewise puts areas of strength for an on frill, with an inclination for things that are striking and eye-getting. Gems is a fundamental part of marvelous style, with explanation pieces like ceiling fixture hoops, sleeve arm bands, and mixed drink rings being well known decisions. Shoes and purses are likewise significant frill, with an inclination for high heels, strappy shoes, and grip sacks.

The variety range of glitzy design is ordinarily rich and striking, with an inclination for gem tones, for example, emerald green, sapphire blue, and ruby red. Metallic shades, for example, gold and silver are likewise well known decisions, as they add a hint of extravagance and marvelousness to any outfit.

One of the principal traits of alluring design is its relationship with Hollywood and the entertainment world. The style arose during the brilliant time of Hollywood, when celebrities like Marilyn Monroe, Elizabeth Taylor, and Audrey Hepburn were commended for their marvelousness and complexity. These famous ladies assisted with advocating fabulous design, and their impact can in any case be found in the style today.

Stylish design has likewise been impacted by other social

developments, for example, the Workmanship Deco development of the 1920s and 30s. Craftsmanship Deco was described by its strong mathematical shapes and unpredictable examples, and these components have been integrated into fabulous style as embellishments like beading and weaving.

As of late, marvelous style has encountered a resurgence in ubiquity, with creators integrating components of the style into their assortments. One of the vital patterns in charming design today is the utilization of metallic textures and embellishments. Metallics add a dash of marvelousness and refinement to any outfit, and they can be consolidated in various ways, from a couple of metallic heels to a sequined skirt.

One more pattern in marvelous design is the utilization of proclamation extras. Strong gems, like larger than usual studs or a thick jewelry, can add a dash of excitement to a generally basic outfit. Essentially, an assertion purse or sets of shoes can hoist a look from conventional to phenomenal.

Stylish design isn't simply restricted to formal events like honorary pathway occasions or weddings. The style can be integrated into regular outfits too, with things, for example, a silk pullover or a velvet coat adding a hint of extravagance to a relaxed look.

All in all, glitzy design is a style that radiates class and refinement, with an emphasis on sumptuous textures, embellishments, and extras. The sign of captivating style is its accentuation on top notch materials and lavish completions, with an inclination for strong varieties and proclamation embellishments. The style arose during the brilliant time of Hollywood and has since turned into a well known style, with fashioners integrating components of the style into their assortments. Whether worn for a conventional event or as a feature of a regular outfit, charming design makes certain to say something and stop people in their tracks.

Sporty

Energetic design is a style that takes motivation from athletic wear and joins it with streetwear components to make an agreeable, easygoing look that is both snappy and utilitarian. The style underscores the utilization of athletic apparel like tennis shoes, running pants, and hoodies, and has become progressively well known as of late as an ever increasing number of individuals take on a functioning way of life.

The sign of energetic style is its accentuation on solace and usefulness. Clothing things are intended to be lightweight and simple to move in, with an emphasis on breathable textures like cotton and polyester. The style likewise underlines layering, with things, for example, hoodies and coats frequently worn over shirts or tank tops.

One of the principal qualities of lively design is the utilization of athletic wear as a style explanation. Tennis shoes are a fundamental part of energetic design, with an inclination for retro-roused styles, for example, Nike Air Max or Adidas Whizzes. These shoes are frequently worn with easygoing outfits like pants or stockings, and can be matched with a hoodie or a plane coat to make an agreeable yet a la mode look.

Notwithstanding tennis shoes, lively style additionally consolidates other athletic wear like workout pants, tights, and sports bras. These things are intended to be worn during active work, yet have likewise become famous as ordinary wear. Stockings, specifically, have turned into a staple of energetic design, with an inclination for high-waisted styles and striking prints.

One more principal attribute of lively design is its consolidation of streetwear components. The style frequently incorporates things, for example, realistic shirts, larger than usual pullovers, and plane coats, which give a gesture to the streetwear tasteful. Extras, for example, baseball covers and knapsacks are likewise famous in lively style, and can add a hint of restlessness to an outfit.

The variety range of lively style is ordinarily intense and splendid, with an inclination for essential tones like red, blue, and yellow. These varieties are in many cases utilized in mix with high contrast to make a striking differentiation. Prints, for example, stripes and camo are likewise well known in lively style, and can be utilized to add a pop of variety or surface to an outfit.

One of the critical patterns in energetic style today is the utilization of reasonable materials. Numerous athletic apparel brands are currently integrating eco-accommodating materials, for example, reused polyester and natural cotton into their attire lines. This pattern mirrors a developing familiarity with the effect that design has on the climate, and a craving to make clothing that is both snappy and maintainable.

As of late, energetic design has likewise become more orientation comprehensive. Many brands are presently making sexually impartial assortments, which are intended to be worn by individuals, all things considered. This pattern mirrors a developing consciousness of the variety of the design business and a longing to make clothing that is open to everybody.

All in all, energetic design is a style that takes motivation from athletic wear and consolidates it with streetwear components to make an agreeable, easygoing look that is both polished and useful. The style underscores the

utilization of active apparel like shoes, warm up pants, and hoodies, and has become progressively famous as of late. The sign of lively design is its accentuation on solace and usefulness, with an inclination for breathable textures and layering. The style likewise integrates streetwear components, for example, realistic shirts and plane coats, and has a strong and splendid variety range. With an emphasis on supportability and inclusivity, lively design is a style that is staying put.

The end.